GROWTH MINDSET WORKSHEETS FOR TEACHERS

PRETTY PICKLES

GET THE MOST OUT OF THIS BOOK

HI THERE! I'M SO GLAD TO SHARE THIS JOURNEY WITH YOU. AFTER YEARS OF RESEARCH, OUR TEAM HAS COME TO LEARN THAT SUCCESS HAS EVERYTHING TO DO WITH A GROWTH MINDSET. WHAT BETTER TIME TO START THAN NOW TO FOSTER SELF-ESTEEM, CONFIDENCE AND SELF-LOVE?

THERE ARE NO RULES WHEN IT COMES TO USING THIS BOOK. FLIP THROUGH THE ACTIVITIES OR DO THEM IN ORDER. HAVE FUN!

MINDSET CHECK-IN

BE KIND TO
YOUR MIND

Changing your mindset

Shifting from a growth mindset to a fixed mindset doesn't happen overnight. Use these questions as a daily reminder to keep growing!

HOW WILL YOU CHALLENGE YOURSELF TODAY?

WHAT CAN YOU DO TO MANAGE CHALLENGES?

WHAT DO YOU WANT TO LEARN TODAY?

WHAT MADE YOU THINK HARD TODAY?

Love is a fruit in season at all times and within reach of every Hand

The Worry Jar

ARE THERE THINGS YOU WORRY ABOUT? RELEASE YOUR
WORRIES BY WRITING THEM DOWN.

You rock!

YOU CAN DO ANYTHING!

You can achieve any goal that you set. Use these writing prompts to guide you through challenges.

My Goal:

List a few challenges you may have to overcome:

List several things you can do to overcome those challenges:

Fill in the blank. When I think I can't achieve this goal, I will....

Fill in the blank. Instead of saying 'I can't' do something, I will...

WHEN I FEEL LIKE I CAN'T OVERCOME A CHALLENGE, I WILL CHAT WITH_______________

YES YOU CAN

REFRAMING YOUR MINDSET

NAME

DATE

The words you use matter

The words you use create your reality. Try reframing the things you say to yourself and watch your world change.

INSTEAD OF SAYING...	SAY THIS INSTEAD...
I can't do this.	i.e. I can do this with a little help.
This is too hard for me.	
Someone else can do a better job.	
This is impossible.	
I give up because I'll never be able to do it.	
It's not going to work out.	
I don't have what it takes to do that...	
I'm not good enough.	

POSITIVE
MIND

POSITIVE
VIBES

POSITIVE
LIFE

MY SUPER POWERS

THINGS I'M GOOD AT

**What
I think I'm good at:**

**What
I want Know I'm good at:**

**What
my friends say I'm good
at:**

SOMETIMES *YOU WIN*

SOMETIMES *YOU LEARN*

Name: Date:

THINGS I'D LIKE TO LEARN

Failure always teaches us the most valuable lessons

Dealing with setbacks

NAME

A SETBACK I'VE EXPERIENCED:

HOW I OVERCAME MY CHALLENGES:

WHAT I COULD HAVE DONE TO COPE BETTER:

NEXT TIME I WILL...

MY MANTRA TO SETBACKS:

SHINE
BRIGHT.
BE
YOURSELF

Books to read

Title of the Book:

Name of the Author:

Title of the Book:

Name of the Author:

Title of the Book:

Name of the Author:

Brief Summary of the Books:

Lessons from the Book:

Actions you'll take after reading these books:

THE
WORLD
IS YOURS TO
CONQUER

If you were a superhero for a day...

If you became a superhero for a day, who would you be? What will be your superpower? Your essay must have at least 350 words and must be written in the first person.

WHAT WE
LEARN
BECOMES A
PART OF WHO
WE ARE

MY SELF PORTRAIT

Draw a picture of yourself.
Highlight your strengths.

Q&A

NOT ALL HEROES
WEAR CAPES

Name

Date

MEET MY HERO

WHO IS YOUR HERO?

Start by answering this question: Who is your hero? Give details about their background, qualities, and achievements. Set up an interview with them.

____

____

____

____

____

____

____

____

____

____

____

Squad Goals

Q+A WITH MY BEST FRIEND

SEE YOURSELF THROUGH SOMEONE ELSE'S EYES

Name   Date

1. What are three words you'd use to describe me?

2. What do you think are my top three strengths?

3. What are three things I can improve on to be a better friend/sibling/child?

LEARNING

IS AN ADVENTURE

Q+A WITH MY MENTOR

SEE YOURSELF THROUGH SOMEONE ELSE'S EYES

Name   Date

1. What are three words you'd use to describe me?

2. What do you think are my top three strengths?

3. What are three things I can improve on to be a better friend/sibling/child?

THERE IS ALWAYS

ROOM TO GROW

Q&A WITH MY MOM

SEE YOURSELF THROUGH SOMEONE ELSE'S EYES

Name   Date

1. What are three words you'd use to describe me?

2. What do you think are my top three strengths?

3. What are three things I can improve on to be a better friend/sibling/child?

YOU ARE

AWESOME

Q+A WITH MY DAD

SEE YOURSELF THROUGH SOMEONE ELSE'S EYES

Name   Date

1. What are three words you'd use to describe me?

2. What do you think are my top three strengths?

3. What are three things I can improve on to be a better friend/sibling/child?

PLAN

ENJOY THE JOURNEY

AROUND THE WORLD

Where would you like to go?

Look at a map and write down the places
you'd like to visit.

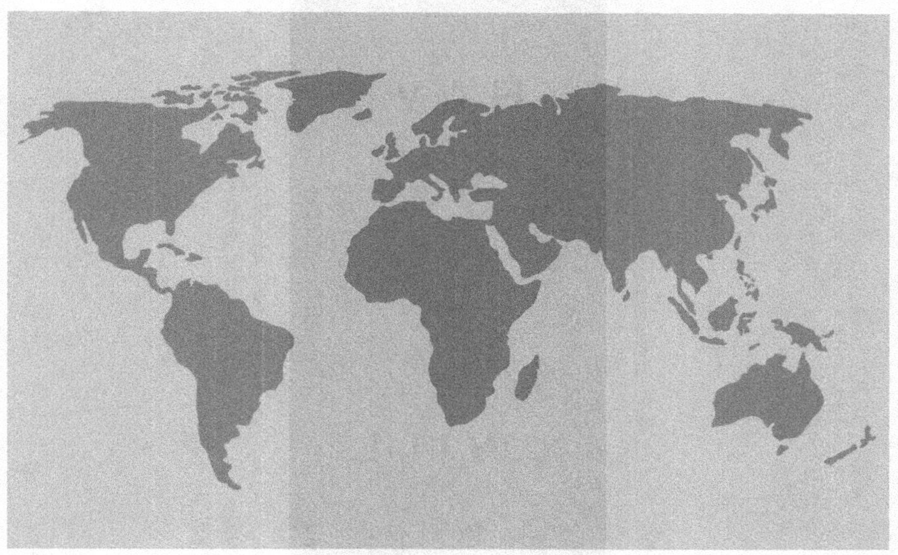

HAVE

PASSPORT

WILL

TRAVEL

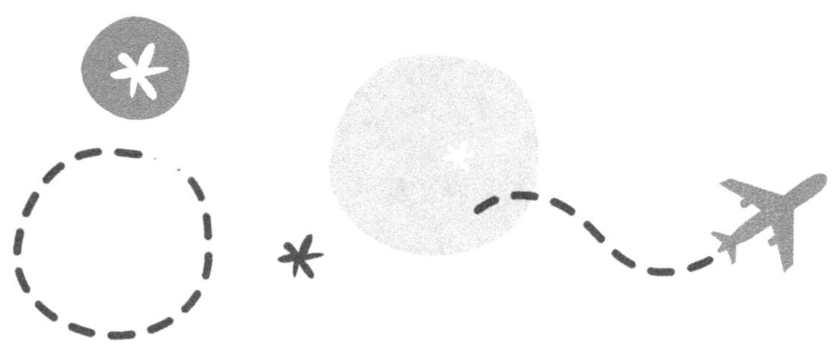

TRAVEL WISHLIST
EXCITED FOR MY NEXT ADVENTURE!

THE CITY AND COUNTRY I WANT TO GO TO NEXT:

THE TIME OF THE YEAR I PLAN TO GO:

THE NUMBER OF DAYS I WILL BE OUT EXPLORING:

THE ACTIVITIES I WANT TO DO ONCE I GET THERE:

FOOD AND DRINKS I WANT TO TRY:

WHO I WANT TO GO WITH ON THIS ADVENTURE:

adventures are forever!

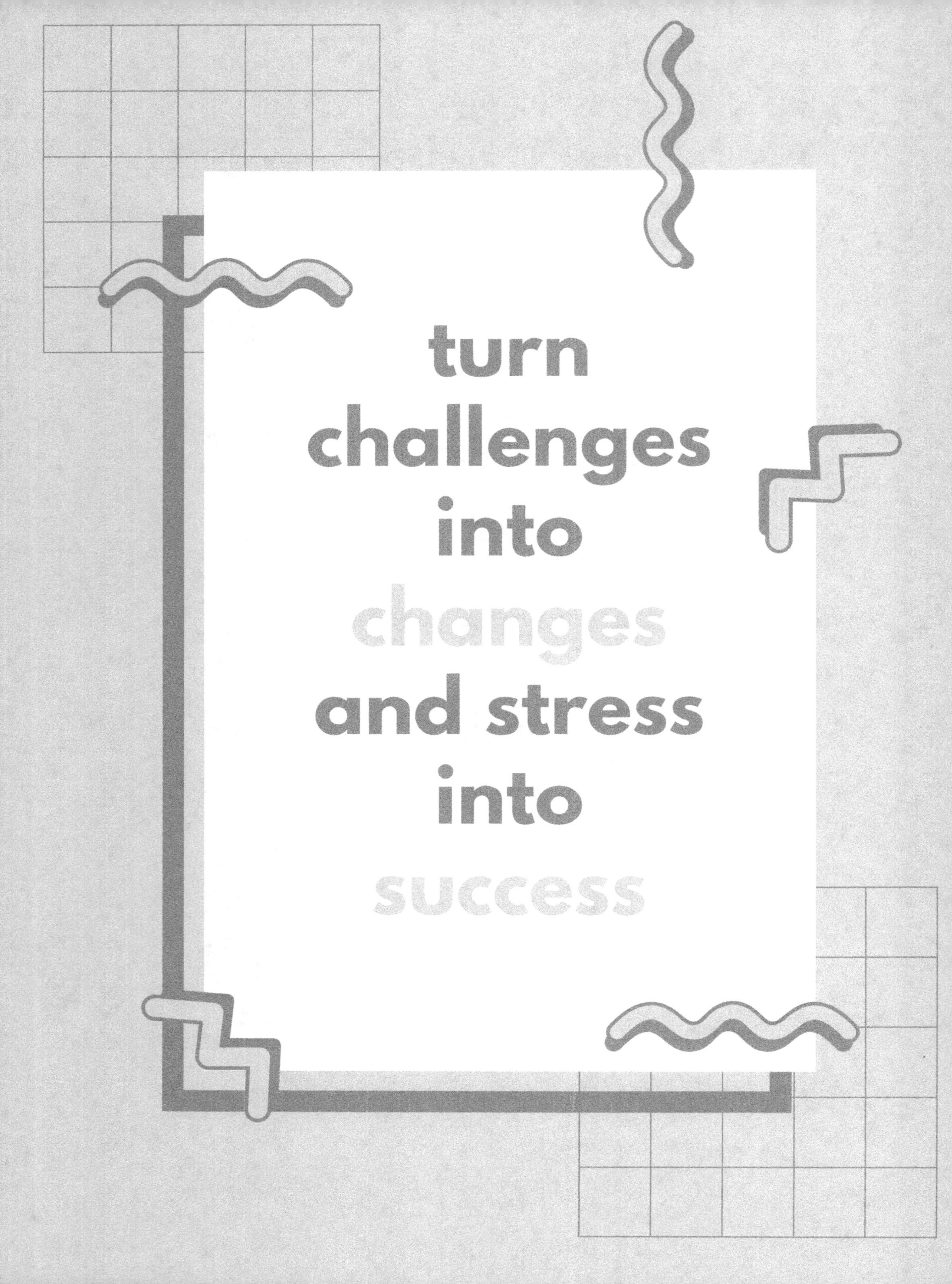
turn
challenges
into
changes
and stress
into
success

THE DAILY ROUTINE

Set up your day for success

TO-DO LIST

MORNING SCHEDULE

AFTERNOON SCHEDULE

DO ALL THINGS WITH
kindness

YOUR
CHORE CHART

CHORE	SU	M	T	W	TH	F	SA

GET
ORGANISED

TO-DOS

DATE & PLACE

MON
____
____

TUE
____
____

WED
____
____

THU
____
____

FRI
____
____

SAT
____
____

SUN
____
____

Seize the day!

All About My Day

Today was a good/bad day for me because...

I was excited to...

I got the opportunity to...

I didn't expect to...

GOALS

You are
AWESOME

ME, MYSELF AND MY GOALS

THE JOB I HOPE TO HAVE ONE DAY:

A PLACE IN THE WORLD I WANT TO LIVE:

A PET I WANT TO HAVE:

A CRAFT I WANT TO LEARN SOON:

A SKILL I WANT TO MASTER:

MY DREAM HOUSE:

NEVER
NEVER
NEVER
GIVE UP

WHAT'S ON MY MIND?

Anything
is
possible.

My top 5 life goals

NEVER
LET GO
OF YOUR
DREAMS

YOUR GOALS

WHAT DO YOU WANT TO ACHIEVE EACH MONTH?

JANUARY	FEBRUARY	MARCH

APRIL	MAY	JUNE

JULY	AUGUST	SEPTEMBER

OCTOBER	NOVEMBER	DECEMBER

PLAY

Make time
for play!

Self - Esteem Bingo

LEARN SOMETHING NEW	LET NEGATIVE PEOPLE GO	DO SOMETHING OUTSIDE YOUR COMFORT ZONE	DO SOMETHING CREATIVE	AFFIRM YOURSELF OFTEN
EXPRESS FEELINGS	ACCEPT FAILURES AS PART OF GROWTH	FACE FEARS	MANAGE TIME WELL	MAKE TIME FOR REST
EXERCISE OFTEN	CULTIVATE HOBBIES	*Free*	LIVE HUMBLY	BE KIND TO YOURSELF
HONOR YOUR WORD TO OTHERS	REMIND YOURSELF YOU ARE ENOUGH	LOVE YOURSELF MORE THAN OTHERS WILL	DREAM BIG AND MAKE IT HAPPEN	CHALLENGE LIMITING BELIEFS
HELP SOMEONE	STOP WORRYING ABOUT WHAT OTHERS THINK	HEAL YOUR PAST	READ SOMETHING INSPIRATIONAL	RECLAIM INTEGRITY

BOOK BINGO

cross out books you've read this
year that showed:

teamwork	motivation	singing & dancing	love
failure and success	a happily ever after	empathy	self-care
grit	an every day hero	self love	overcoming obstacles
a growth mindset	a valuable lesson	a healthy relationship	self-love

THE SIX MONTH PLAN

GROWTH MINDSET PLAN MONTH 1

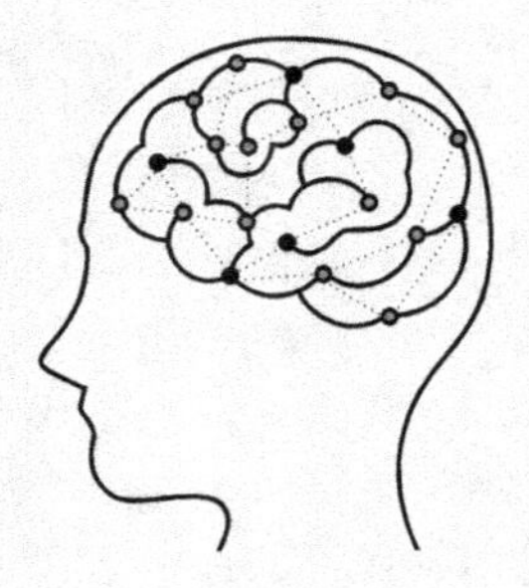

ONE THING YOU'LL DO DAILY

	WEEK 1	WEEK 2	WEEK 3	WEEK 4
MON	i.e. Learn a new skill			
TUE				
WED				
THU				
FRI				

GROWTH MINDSET PLAN MONTH 2

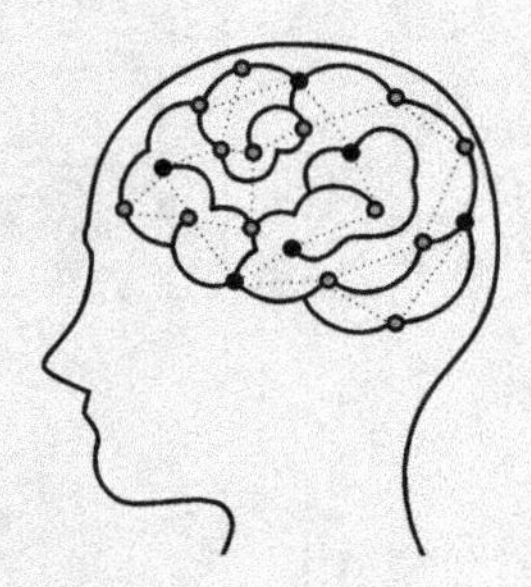

ONE THING YOU'LL DO DAILY

	WEEK 1	WEEK 2	WEEK 3	WEEK 4
MON	i.e. Learn a new skill			
TUE				
WED				
THU				
FRI				

GROWTH MINDSET PLAN MONTH 3

ONE THING YOU'LL DO DAILY

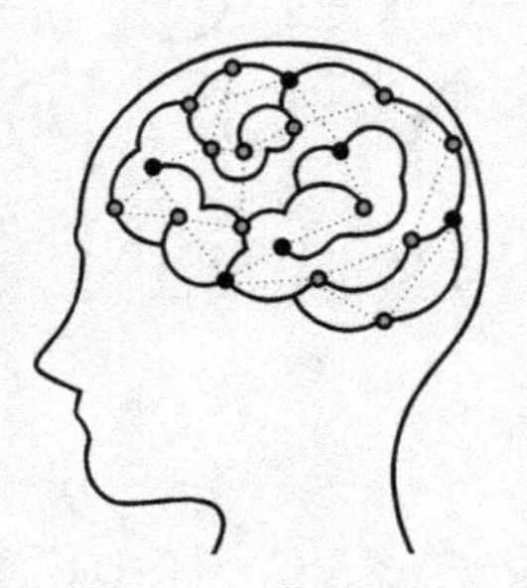

	WEEK 1	WEEK 2	WEEK 3	WEEK 4
MON	i.e. Learn a new skill			
TUE				
WED				
THU				
FRI				

GROWTH MINDSET PLAN MONTH 4

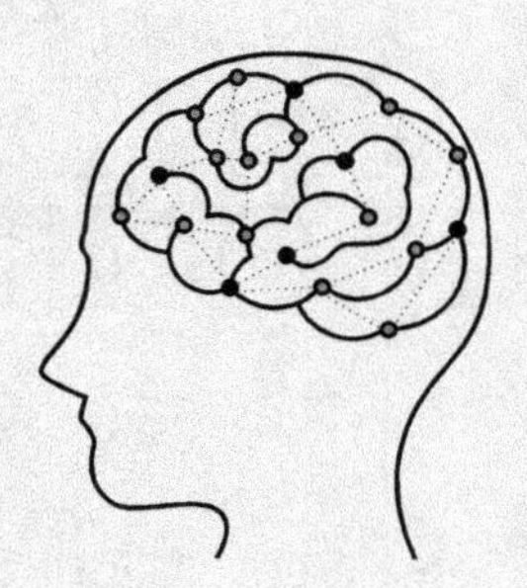

ONE THING YOU'LL DO DAILY

	WEEK 1	WEEK 2	WEEK 3	WEEK 4
MON	i.e. Learn a new skill			
TUE				
WED				
THU				
FRI				

GROWTH MINDSET PLAN MONTH 5

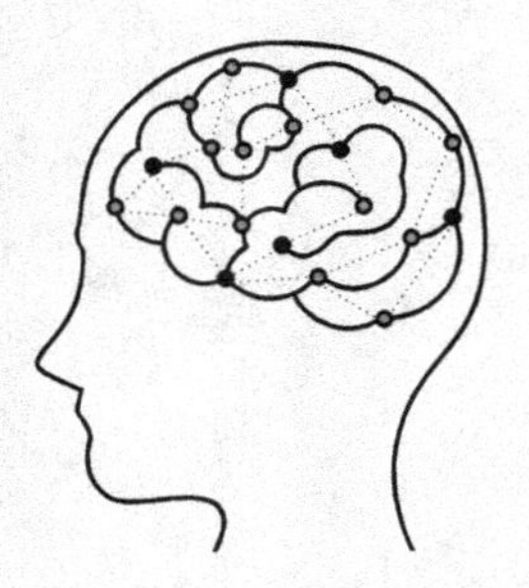

ONE THING YOU'LL DO DAILY

	WEEK 1	WEEK 2	WEEK 3	WEEK 4
MON	i.e. Learn a new skill			
TUE				
WED				
THU				
FRI				

GROWTH MINDSET PLAN MONTH 6

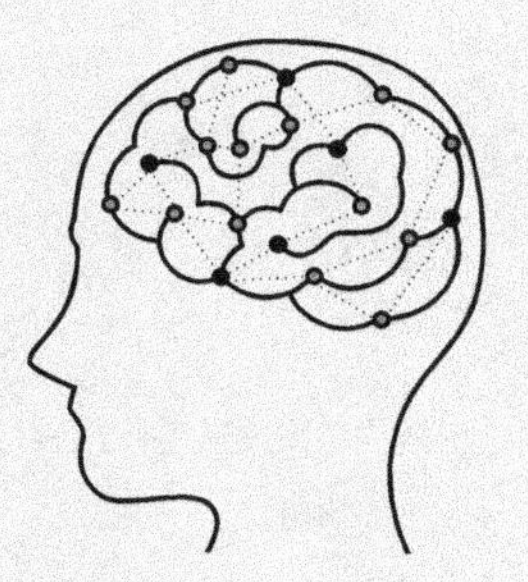

ONE THING YOU'LL DO DAILY

	WEEK 1	WEEK 2	WEEK 3	WEEK 4
MON	i.e. Learn a new skill			
TUE				
WED				
THU				
FRI				

REFLECTION

MY REFLECTION ESSAY

NAME

DATE

Write an essay based on this prompt:

Write about a time when you were told you couldn't do something. Did you believe it? How did it make you feel? What will you do the next time you're told you can't do something?

MY REFLECTION ESSAY

NAME

DATE

Write an essay based on this prompt:

What is one of the most challenging days you've had. Address the steps you took to overcome the challenge and what you learned from it.

MY REFLECTION ESSAY

Write an essay based on this prompt:

Think about one of the biggest mistakes you've ever made. What did you gain from it? What did you learn?

MY REFLECTION ESSAY

NAME

DATE

Write an essay based on this prompt:

Think about a time when you accomplished something that you didn't think you could. What were three things you learned?

MY REFLECTION ESSAY

Write an essay based on this prompt:

Write about one of your long-term goals. What is the goal and what are you doing each day to make sure you accomplish that goal?

NOTES

MUSIC THAT INSPIRES YOU

MUSIC THAT INSPIRES YOU

BOOKS THAT INSPIRE YOU

BOOKS THAT INSPIRE YOU

PLACES THAT INSPIRE YOU

PLACES THAT INSPIRE YOU

FOOD THAT INSPIRE YOU

RANDOM THOUGHTS

RANDOM THOUGHTS

RANDOM THOUGHTS